The WILSON LINE

The statue of Charles Henry Wilson, Lord Nurburnholme, (1833-1907) in Alfred Street, Hull.

The WILSON LINE

Arthur G. Credland

TEMPUS

First published 2000
Copyright © Arthur G. Credland, 2000

Tempus Publishing Limited
The Mill, Brimscombe Port,
Stroud, Gloucestershire, GL5 2QG

ISBN 0 7524 1728 2

Typesetting and origination by
Tempus Publishing Limited
Printed in Great Britain by
Midway Clark Printing, Wiltshire

Wilson vessels tied up at the Riverside Quay, Hull, c.1954, dominated by the landmark clock tower. The SS *Gitano*, fitted with two steam turbines by Earles of Hull, was launched at Goole in 1921. After a bunker fire in 1955 she was sold for breaking, as was the *Urbino* (behind) the previous year.

Contents

Acknowledgements

My very great thanks to Gertrude Attwood whose knowledge of the Wilsons of Tranby Croft is boundless. Thanks also due to to Ben Chapman for a delightful photograph from his personal archive, Graham Edwards for preparation of many of the photographs, the staff of the Hull Local Studies Library, J.R. (Bob) Fewlass, Mike Thompson and not least Joanne Hall and Lisa Stokes, who prepared the typescript from my hideous scrawl.

The volume and all royalties are dedicated to the Hull Maritime Society who have enthusiastically supported the Hull Maritime Museum over the last quarter of a century.

Other than the exceptions referred to, all images are from the Museum's Wilson collection.

Introduction

Thomas Wilson, founder of the line, was born at Hull in 1792, the son of a lighterman, and baptized at the Dagger Lane Independent Chapel on 14 February the same year. He was apprenticed as a clerk in the counting house of Whitaker, Wilkinson, who were importers of Swedish iron, and was eventually appointed as their traveller in the Sheffield district. Marriage to Susannah West in 1814 and a rapidly growing family led, according to the traditional story handed down, to a request for a rise in pay – which was refused. Wilson then resigned and set up on his own account in the iron-importing business. Initially cargoes were loaded on ships owned by others but the extra capital brought by a John Beckinton enabled the new firm of Beckinton, Wilson & Co. to charter and eventually purchase vessels of its own. Additional partners, John Hudson (a Hull druggist) and Thomas Hudson, gentleman of Newcastle, were shareholders in the *Swift*, a wooden schooner acquired in 1831, the first vessel Wilson was directly involved in owning. In 1836, Beckinton withdrew and the firm became known as Wilson, Hudson & Co. with its offices at 14 Salthouse Lane. Wilson also lived there in some style, according to a reminiscence of Thomas Brooks (carver and gilder): 'when a boy, my mother took me in a sedan chair to a ball at Mr Wilson's home in Salthouse Lane.' The address was a convenient one, not only because of the nearness to the town docks, but it was also next door to the Hull branch of the Bank of England.

The Hudsons withdrew in 1841 and the business became a purely family affair, titled Thomas Wilson, Sons & Co. The three eldest sons David, Edward and John were all active in the organisation. John West Wilson, who established an agency in Gothenburg, being for several years a master in the Wilson fleet. Specialisation in iron imports had been abandoned and all kinds of cargoes were transported to and fro across the North Sea.

Availability of subsidies (between 1840 and 1842) from the Norwegian and Swedish governments for carrying mail led Wilson to charter several steam-powered vessels, his first involvement with steamships. In 1851, the *Courier*, a paddle steamer, was the first steamer actually purchased for the fleet. David Wilson left the company in 1858 to concentrate on running the wine and spirit business established by his maternal grandfather. By 1861 an ageing Thomas Wilson had relinquished his holding into the hands of Charles Henry and Arthur Wilson, the two younger sons. They continued to develop the Norwegian trade and, when the father died in 1869, embarked on an expansion programme, which was to make Wilsons a truly international line.

Poster design for the SS *Eskimo*, built at Earles shipyard in Hull for the Scandinavian trade and employed for summer cruises along the Norway coast.

The temporary closure of the Prussian ports during the Franco-Prussian war of 1870-1871 led to transfer of vessels to Trieste and the start of a vigorous Adriatic trade which later extended to Sicily. Opening of the Suez Canal in 1869, the year Thomas died, enabled vessels to avoid the long route around the Cape and in 1871 the SS *Orlando* sailed to Bombay, quickly followed by the SS *Thomas Wilson*. Excessive competition terminated this venture until the 1880s but in 1875 the *Othello* was transferred from the Indian to the North American run, a bold effort since the transatlantic trade was dominated by the well established Liverpool shipowners. Wilsons cleverly forced the American brokers to offer cargoes after first bypassing them; Wilsons acting as their own merchants, brokers and shippers and took a threefold profit. By the 1890s, Wilson vessels were carrying more cargo to and from New York than those of any other fleet, with passages from Hull, the Tyne and London as well as Gothenburg, Stettin and Copenhagen. A not insignificant element in the success of the trade were the high quality steamships built at Earles shipyard in Hull with their powerful and fuel-efficient compound and triple-expansion engines.

Emigrants were an important part of the company's business. Large numbers of Norwegians and Swedes escaping economic depression and Jewish refugees of the Tsarist pogroms were brought into Hull. Most were put on the railway and transported to Liverpool to take ship for America but some stayed in Hull and others helped to develop the Jewish communities in Manchester and Leeds (helping the latter to become a major centre of ready-to-wear tailoring).

The year 1891 saw Thomas Wilson & Sons become a private limited company with share capital of £2 million, with all but 900 of the £100 shares in the hands of Charles and Arthur Wilson. Earles shipyard was purchased by Charles in 1901 after it had gone into voluntary liquidation, the result of persistent labour problems. He paid £150,000 and invested a further £170,000 of new capital to restart operations. It may be noted that up to the First World War almost half the output of the yard was for the Wilson Line.

Two years later the entire Bailey and Leetham steamer fleet (twenty-three vessels), offices and engineering facilities were acquired for £350,000, a bargain since an estimate of the full value was nearly double that. Both these Hull lines had been suffering from competition in the Scandinavian and Baltic trade from Det Forenede Dampskibs Selskab (DFDS) of Copenhagen. Wilson's Oswald Sanderson, soon to become managing director – and with a fleet of nearly a hundred ships – was now negotiating from strength and signed an agreement which divided the gross profits of vessels run between Hull and Copenhagen and Hull–Windau, with equal sailings on the London, Copenhagen, Konigsberg route. The two firms were also to be exclusive agents for each other and close links persisted through two world wars when Wilsons managed DFDS vessels seized by the British authorities.

In 1906, after thirty-two years as a Liberal MP for Hull, Charles Henry Wilson was ennobled as the first Lord Nunburnholme of Warter Priory, a title taken from his country estate in East Yorkshire. Sadly he did not have long to enjoy his new status and died on 27 October 1907. His brother (a Conservative in politics) was never tempted to seek a parliamentary seat and, instead, was active in the social life of the county, especially as an enthusiastic Master of the Holderness Hunt. He was also Sheriff of Hull from 1888-1889 and High Sheriff of Yorkshire in 1891. Arthur's wife Mary and his daughters revelled in the life of the 'county set' and the 'high society' which enjoyed their hospitality both in Grosvenor Place, their London home, and at Tranby Croft on the western outskirts of Hull. Two years after his brother, Arthur died of stomach cancer and his son, Edward Kenneth Wilson, succeeded him as chairman, though

A postcard of RMS *Oslo*. Launched at Earles shipyard in 1906, she had a length of 290ft and a displacement of 2,296 tons gross, with accommodation for ninety-five first class, thirty-two second class and up to 400 steerage passengers. She was torpedoed off Shetland in August 1917 by U-87 while on a run from Trondheim to Liverpool carrying passengers and copper ore.

the managing director, Oswald Sanderson, was now the real driving force in the company. Charles' son, the second Lord Nunburnholme, now vice-chairman, was frequently at loggerheads with Sanderson and eventually persuaded the rest of the family to sell. Losses from the fleet in the First World War were considerable – shippers of neutral nations were taking full advantage of the situation and, in addition, the rumblings of revolution in Russia were bound to affect trade with the Baltic states.

An offer of £4.1 million was therefore accepted from Sir John Reeves Ellerman, with Oswald Sanderson remaining managing director and Ellerman himself becoming chairman. Now styled Ellerman's Wilson Line, it remained independent of the rest of the Ellerman empire and this special status probably resulted from Ellerman's personal connection with Hull. He was born there in 1862 (at 100 Anlaby Road), although he left the city as a young boy of seven.

Rebuilding the fleet was a priority after the end of hostilities but trading conditions were desperately difficult. Too many ships were chasing the available cargoes. Earles shipyard was shut down in 1932 as a result of the Depression and a scarcity of orders.

The Second World War resulted in a reduction of the fleet from thirty-five vessels to just nine and another rebuilding programme got under way in 1945. Business was buoyant in the 1950s, but the break-up of the Empire and the emergence of new shipping nations, often paying much lower wages to their personnel, made it increasingly difficult to compete. The once-lucrative North American trade finished in 1961 but a determined effort was made to improve cargo-handling efficiency and lower labour costs with the S-class boats, starting with the *Salerno* in 1965. Then in the following year, the hugely ambitious and expensive *Spero* was launched as part of an EWL and Scandinavian consortium to operate the Gothenburg route. She was Hull's first roll-on-roll-off vessel but the volume of trade and the numbers of passengers and cars were much below expectations.

Two ro-ro vessels, *Destro* and *Domino*, were launched for the Scandinavian trade and entered service in 1970 and 1972 respectively. The *Spero* was transferred to the Hull-Zeebrugge run, accompanied by a massive publicity campaign to try to attract a large volume of passengers for mini-cruises to the continent (starting at £13.50!).

J.R. Fewlass was the last chairman of Ellerman's Wilson Line and after his death in 1959 the company became a wholly owned subsidiary of Ellerman Lines, London.

1972 saw a major reorganisation of Ellerman Lines which moved entirely away from the old company identities –with largely self-contained operations – to a divisional arrangement. Ellerman City Lines controlling shipping, EWL was concerned with transport and Ellerman Travel and Leisure was the other division.

Hero, jointly owned by EWL and DFDS and used on the Hull-Esbjerg service, was lost off Heligoland in November 1977 and expensive charters had to be made to take the place of this profitable vessel. In 1978, the departure of *Destro* from King George dock, Hull, on 29 September under the command of Captain Frank Barnes, senior master, proved to be the last Wilson vessel to work from the port of Hull. In 1983, the entire Ellerman Group was up for sale with recent losses of £9 million. Bought by the hoteliers David and Frederick Barclay, the shipping component was subsequently acquired in a management buy-out in 1985, and two years later sold to Trafalgar House plc (owners of Cunard) to create Cunard Ellerman. In 1991 P&O purchased the Ellerman Group container business and sold the four remaining ships to Andrew Weir Shipping Ltd.

The Wilson name now only survives in Sweden as Wilson and Co. (shipping agents), of Gothenburg. Here in Hull, the old offices in Commercial Road no longer resound to the clamour of telephones and busy shipping clerks. Instead, the gentle click of 'woods' making contact can be heard in the indoor bowling green that now occupies the main hall!

Arthur G. Credland, Hull Maritime Museum, January 2000

One

Thomas Wilson & Sons
The Early Years

Park House, Cottingham, near Hull, *c.*1867. Thomas Wilson, his wife and five daughters stand outside their home. Born on 12 February 1792, the son of a lighterman, he married Susannah West, daughter of a wine and spirit merchant, on 1 September 1814.

Schooners *Dwina* and *Ellen Crawford*, c.1841. Aged about thirty, with experience as a representative of a firm of iron merchants, he teamed up with John Beckinton who provided the capital to set up an iron importing business. Initially chartering vessels, in 1831 they bought the wooden schooner *Swift* and, in 1841, in partnership with R.M. Sawyer and Charles and George Cammell, purchased the *Dwina*. Charles Cammell, iron founder of Sheffield, later established the famous shipbuilding firm of Cammell Laird.

The Dock, Hull, c.1811. A view of the city's first enclosed dock, opened in 1778. William Westerdale, mast, block and pump maker, welcomes guests aboard the *Wellington*, newly fitted out. The church on the left is St. Johns, demolished in the 1920s to make way for the Ferens Art Gallery.

Salthouse Lane, 1888; a drawing by F.S. Smith. The Sailors Home, No.13, was originally the Hull branch of the Bank of England. Wilson's home and shipping office was next door, at No.14, just outside the drawing and now demolished. It was conveniently close to the docks and all the activity of the old town area.

SS *North Sea*, 1855. The first twelve vessels in the Wilson fleet were all wooden sailing vessels but 1851 saw the purchase of the iron paddle steamer *Courier*. The *North Sea*, an iron screw steamer, was built by Earles of Hull in 1855 and was the beginning of a long association with that shipyard. She was 208ft (63m) long and 662 tons gross, powered by a single two-cylinder engine.

SS *Atlantic* 1857. The *North Sea* was followed by the *Neva* (1856), *Kingston* (1856) and then the *Atlantic*, all built at Earles shipyard. She sailed for Wilsons until 1874, then sold to J. Moss of Liverpool and in Turkish ownership as the *Kaplan* was lost in a collision on passage from Heraklea to the Dardanelles in 1898.

The *Oder* and the *Ouse*, 1862. Both vessels were built by Earles, the former in 1861 and the latter the following year. Passage across the North Sea and navigation in the Baltic, though not a long distance, provided plenty of navigation hazards. The *Oder* was lost in 1875 sailing from Liverpool to Gothenburg with general cargo and the *Ouse* was wrecked off Jutland in fog in 1867 while carrying general cargo from Hull to Stettin.

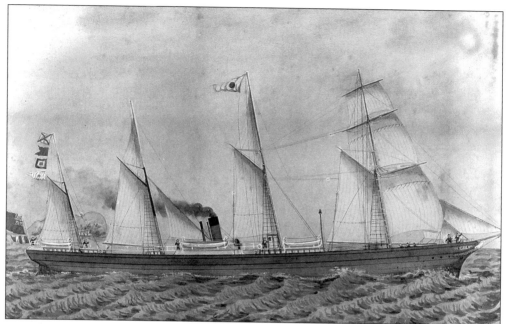

SS *Dido*, 1862. Also built by C.&W. Earle, this iron-hulled ship with clipper bow was 278ft (85m) long and 1,342 tons gross. She has the 'o' ending to her name which became characteristic of the Wilson line, starting with the *Argo* in 1860. Note the house flag which was a white pennant with red ball.

SS *Calypso*, 1865. Yet another Earles-built vessel, the twentieth from that yard to join the fleet, she was 251ft (80m) long and 1,337 tons gross. The *Calypso* remained in service for thirty-seven years and was broken up at Genoa in 1902.

Thomas Wilson (1792-1869); a portrait probably engraved to commemorate his death on 21 June 1869. He relinquished active involvement in the firm in 1858 leaving the younger brothers Charles and Arthur as the principals. At the end of 1869, the *Orlando*, launched by Earles, became the fifty-seventh vessel to serve in the Wilson fleet.

Albert Dock, Hull 1869. The year of the founder's death saw the opening of a new dock, named in honour of the Prince Consort by the Prince of Wales on July 22. Here the royal party boards the PS *Vivid*, a vessel belonging to the Humber Union Steam Packet Company. An event of world importance for the expansion of trade was the opening of the Suez Canal in that same year. This allowed vessels to reach the Far East without the long voyage around the Cape of Good Hope, at the tip of Africa.

Two
The Second
Generation: Expansion

S.S. THOMAS WILSON.

SS *Thomas Wilson* painted in 1892. One of the first ships launched for the two sons was named in honour of their late father. Built in 1870, yet again, by Earles she was a long-serving vessel and was sold in 1901 to a company in Riga. She foundered in the North Sea in November 1909, sailing from Riga to Antwerp. The crew were rescued and landed at Hull by a Norwegian steamer.

SS *Rollo* was launched at Earles shipyard in 1870 and was 260ft (79m) long and 1,437 tons gross. In regular service to Gothenburg frequently carrying emigrants from Scandinavia and the Baltic States, the *Rollo* had accommodation for fifty first class, twenty-eight second class and 498 steerage passengers. Brought into Hull, migrants boarded westbound trains, most eventually taking ship from Liverpool to the USA.

Wilson and Co, Jarntoget, Gothenburg, *c.*1925. John West Wilson (1816-1889), the second son, was the firm's agent in Sweden and in 1843 set up his own company which exists to this day. J.W. Wilson took Swedish citizenship and died unmarried overseas.

David Wilson (1815-1893). The eldest son left direct involvement in the shipping firm before his father's death. He had succeeded to the wine and spirit business established by his maternal grandfather.

The Wilson offices, 1 Commercial Row. Situated at the junction with Kingston Street, these purpose-built premises were opened in 1873 to accommodate the rapidly expanding company. The tall windows illuminate the main hall where the myriad clerks attended to the never-ending mass of ships papers, tickets, bills, receipts, etc.

Clerks in the main hall, *c*.1890. This large, well-lit room rose to the full height of two floors. Later a mezzanine was installed giving access to the second floor offices adjoining.

SS *Hindoo*, 1872, a painting by Samuel Walters, marine artist of Liverpool. Taking advantage of the Suez Canal the *Orlando* sailed to Bombay in 1871 and the *Thomas Wilson* began the Calcutta service. The *Colombo*, *Hindoo* and *Othello* were all launched in 1872 and entered the trade to India. *Hindoo* was 380ft (116m) long and 3,257 tons gross. Spacious accommodation for first and second class passengers was fully ventilated for tropical conditions.

Commercial Road, c.1880; looking northward with Wilson's premises at the corner, on the right. Adjoining the offices to the east was Railway Dock. Opened in 1846 this modest-sized basin some three acres (twelve hectares) was monopolised by the Wilson line after the opening of their new headquarters.

SS *Zebra* c.1878. Newer, larger vessels were put into the long distance services so the purchase of the Brownlow Marsdin fleet in 1878 provided seven steamers for the North Sea services. Brownlow Pearson, their predecessors and managers of Hull's first steamship firm, the Hull Steam Packet Co., had built the *Zebra* in 1859 but she remained in service with Wilsons till 1894; she was 196ft (60m) long and 551 tons gross.

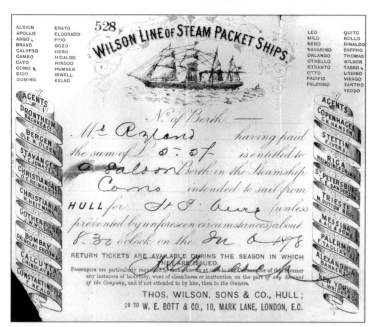

Wilson steamship ticket. A rare surviving example of a nineteenth century steamer ticket, dated 6 June 1878 for a saloon berth aboard SS *Como* from Hull to St Petersburg, for five guineas. The ticket lists the entire fleet of forty-one vessels and agents in all the regular ports of call. William Eagle Bott married Harriet, one of Thomas Wilson's daughters.

Amos and Smith's engine shop. In 1874, Arthur Wilson formed a partnership with Charles Frederick Amos and his brother-in-law, Henry Wilson Ringrose Smith, to found Amos and Smith, marine engineers. When Smith died in 1890 his interest was purchased by Charles Henry Wilson.

Hull Corporation Pier and the Humber dock basin, c.1900. The pier was used by the Humber paddle ferries sailing between Hull and New Holland, Lincs. A steamer is moored to the eastern side of the basin, another, seen in profile is tied up inside. The Railway Dock, at right angles to the Humber Dock entered it on its western side; together these now form the Hull Marina.

SS *Colorado*, 1887. In 1875 Wilsons were confident enough to enter the transatlantic trade and soon cornered a significant niche in the North American trade despite the long-established presence of the Liverpool companies. A major factor in their success were the high quality ships built at Earles shipyard and particularly their powerful and fuel-efficient, triple expansion steam engines, among the finest ever made.

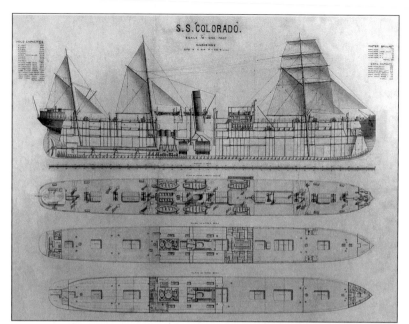

SS *Colorado*, 1890. A handsomely drawn general arrangement plan of this transatlantic steamer. She was built by Earles Shipbuilding & Engineering Co. in 1887 and was sold for breaking in 1907 after twenty years ploughing the seas between Britain and America.

The 'black gang' – engine room crew of SS *Colorado*; photographed in New York, 9 February 1897. The vessel was 370ft (113m) long and 4,220 tons gross with a triple expansion steam engine of 508 nominal horsepower.

SS *Buffalo*. Launched by Palmers of Jarrow, Newcastle-on-Tyne, she made her maiden voyage to New York from the Tyne on 6 November 1885. This painting was made by Antonio Jacobsen, marine painter of Hoboken, New Jersey, in 1886.

Norway service 1897; notice advertising a special rail connection from Kings Cross, London, to Hull to board the Wilson mail steamer *Eldorado* for summer cruises along the Norwegian coast, with stops at Stavanger and Bergen.

Charles Henry Wilson photographed on 26 October 1896. Born in 1833 he and his younger brother Arthur were the principals of the Wilson Line and took the company to heights undreamt of by their father who had concentrated on the established North Sea routes. He was elected as a liberal Member of Parliament for Hull in 1874 and was ennobled as Lord Nunburnholme in 1906.

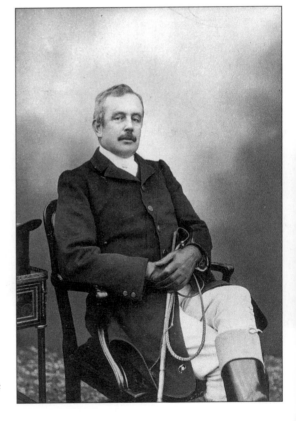

Arthur Wilson c.1878. The younger son, born in 1836, like his brother became the owner of a large mansion, and some 3,000 acres of land. In 1878, he became master of the Holderness Hunt, a costly exercise which was said to have absorbed some £4,000 a year in the 1890s. His status as M.F.H. confirmed his place in local society and he entertained lavishly at his home, Tranby Croft, on the western side of the city.

Three
The Baccarat Scandal
and a Dock Strike

TRANBY CROFT.

Tranby Croft, home of Arthur Wilson. On 1 July 1863 he had married, at Leeds Parish Church, Mary Emma Smith daughter of E.J. Smith, who was then the Leeds City Postmaster but had previously been Army Postmaster during the Crimean War. The couple at first occupied a fine Georgian house in the centre of Hull but in May 1874; an infant Arthur Stanley Wilson laid the foundation stone for their new house which was completed in 1876.

Dining room, Tranby Croft, 1900. Elaborate overmantels, panelling, paintings, ornaments and comfortable upholstery combine to create a lush interior.

Drawing room, Tranby Croft. The potted palms, an abundance of chairs, occasional tables and cases with crockery and ornaments yield a typical Victorian effect of cluttered comfort. There were sixty rooms in the three-story mansion but, within ten years of building, a whole new wing was added making a total of over a hundred rooms.

Holderness Hunt at Tranby Croft 18 January 1907. Arthur and Mary Wilson made the most of their fine new house and, with his position as Master of the Holderness Hunt, they were able to play a leading role in 'county' society. Tranby attracted a large number of titled ladies and gentlemen, performers such as Nelly Melba and literary lions, notably Oscar Wilde.

House Party at Tranby Croft. In 1889, Prince Albert Edward Victor (the Duke of Clarence), the Prince of Wales' eldest son, usually known as Eddie, made his first visit; here seen third from the left on the front row clasping a cane. Standing behind him is Arthur Stanley (Jack) Wilson and in the middle of the front row enveloped in fur is Mary Wilson. On the extreme left is Ethel Lycett Green, Arthur and Mary's daughter.

Billiard Room, Tranby Croft. On 8 September 1890, the Prince of Wales and a party which included his equerry and Lord Edward Somerset arrived to stay, conveniently placed to take train for Doncaster and the St. Leger race meeting. After a large dinner and singing by Ethel Lycett Green, the Prince of Wales asked to play a game of baccarat. This was continued the next evening in the billiard room which was to be the scene of the much debated Baccarat Scandal.

Edward, Prince of Wales (1841-1910); Queen Victoria's heir, a noted *bon viveur* and womaniser, his increasingly portly figure led to him being called 'Tum-Tum' among his circle of intimates. He and Sir William Gordon Cumming, the victim of the Baccarat Scandal, had both competed for the favours of Daisy Brooke, Countess of Warwick.

Drawing room, Tranby Croft. On the fateful evening of 9 September, young 'Jack' Wilson thought he saw Colonel Cumming cheating and told his brother-in-law Edward Lycett Green (son of a Wakefield iron master). Confronted with the accusation, the Colonel claimed he was using a betting system the inexperienced young men were unfamiliar with. It was agreed that the affair would be kept quiet as long as he agreed never to play cards again.

At the Old Bailey 1891. From left to right; the Judge, Lord Coleridge, Prince of Wales and Col. Cumming. Unfortunately, word of the allegations got out and Col. Cumming had to resort to law in an attempt to clear his name. He brought an action against 'Jack' Wilson, his mother Mary, the Lycett Greens and Jack's friend Berkeley Levett. Much to Queen Victoria's chagrin the Prince of Wales was called to give evidence as a material witness, especially embarrassing since Baccarat was an illegal gambling game in Britain.

Mary Wilson being cross-examined by Sir Edward Clarke, the lawyer leading the case for Sir William Gordon Cumming. The trial began on 1 June 1891 and lasted for nine days.

Mr Gill cross-examining

Sketches in court from the *Illustrated London News*, June 13th, 1891

Illustrated London News 13 June 1891. The trial filled the newspapers and magazines. Here we have from left to right, top to bottom; 'Jack' Wilson, General Sir Owen Williams, Lord Coventry, Mr Asquith QC (acting for the defendants), a juror asking a question, Lord Edward Somerset, Mr Gill (junior to Sir Edward Clarke), and Berkeley Levett.

Lt Col. Sir William Gordon Cumming. On 9 June the jury reached their verdict in only thirteen minutes and found for the defendants. Effectively Gordon-Cumming was branded a cheat, forced to resign his colonelcy and retire from society to his Scottish estates. On the day after the trial he married an American heiress! Dispassionate consideration of the evidence would suggest he had been wrongly accused by inexperienced young men unfamiliar with the nuances of the game.

MISS A. CROFT & BABY BEECROFT.

Annie Croft, a foundling, was apparently left at Tranby Croft *c.*1892, hence her surname. She became a notable West End actress and review artist. Her youngest son, David Croft, made his stage debut aged twelve in 1934 and has since achieved fame as co-writer with Jimmy Perry, of *Dads Army*, the television saga of the Home Guard. It may be noted he named one of the principals (Sgt) Arthur Wilson!

Hull High School for Girls. The notoriety of the Tranby Croft affair did not impede Arthur Wilson's progress and, while the public were agog with the events, he was appointed High Sheriff of Yorkshire. 'Jack' Wilson was admitted to the Marlborough Club on the recommendation of the Prince of Wales! Since 1944 Tranby Croft has been the Hull High School for Girls. Gordon Cumming's home at Gordonstown was sold to Kurt Hahn, the educationist, to become a celebrated school where both Prince Philip and Prince Charles were pupils!

Dock Strike at Hull, April 1893. Arthur Wilson had not much time to dwell on the events of the Prince of Wales' visit. He was a busy public figure but above all a dedicated businessman involved with his brother in running an outstandingly successful shipping line. Here Wilson clerks roll up their sleeves to unload the firm's steamers in Railway Dock.

Dock Strike at Hull, 1893. Here the clerks, of all ages and sizes, pose for the camera. Note the figure with arms folded, second from right, second row, his docker's hook tucked into his belt and sporting a cricket or rugby cap.

Dock Strike at Hull, 1893. Feelings ran high between the union men and the strike breakers and there were outbreaks of arson on Victoria Dock. Here, a contingent of the 2nd Dragoons patrol the quayside to prevent any further damage.

Halifax Detachment on Duty at Hull Dockers' Strike, 1893.

Dock Strike at Hull, 1893. The strike lasted seven weeks and police were drafted in from all over the North of England, this is the Halifax detachment posed on board the Wilson steamer *Hidalgo*. A local gunsmith reported selling more than 200 revolvers but only one person, one of the strikers, was reported injured by shooting.

Hull, *c.*1906. Monument Bridge passed between the Princes and Queens docks. The column is a monument to William Wilberforce, the Emancipator, and the building with dome and clock is the former headquarters of the Hull Dock Company and then the NER, which bought the Hull docks in 1893. It now houses the city's Maritime Museum.

Details of Bird's Eye View 1881. The river Hull flows north to south into the Humber. The Town Docks, i.e. Humber Dock, Princes Dock and Queens Dock (the first enclosed dock, 1778) form an arc joining the Humber to the Hull, following the line of the old city walls. The 'island' surrounded by water represents the extent of the 'old town' before its expansion in the eighteenth century.

City of London Imperial volunteers boarding SS *Ariosto*, 1900. Though Charles Henry Wilson was a Liberal MP, and an opponent of the Boer War, his patriotism was never in doubt and he gave the government the use of the *Toronto* and *Ariosto* free of charge for carrying troops to Cape Town. After the reverses of 1899, the arrival of the volunteer regiments recovered the initiative.

SS *Ariosto*. Launched at Earles shipyard in 1889, 300ft (91m) long and 2,376 tons gross she was first put in the Hull-Gothenburg trade. Sold to a Spanish company in 1910 she was sunk by a German submarine in 1916, not far from Bishop Rock, while on passage from Valencia to Liverpool with fruit and vegetables.

Capt. Newman, 1900. Master of the *Ariosto*, posing on deck resplendent with walrus moustache and side whiskers.

Capt. Page of the *Galileo*, 1896. In February 1896, she managed to tow the steamer *Oceanic* into Boston harbour after the propeller shaft had been broken in heavy weather. Belonging to the Britannic Steamship Company of Sunderland, all twenty-four crew and their master, Captain Gibson, were saved.

Captain G.R.W. Bray and stewardesses. He first became master of the SS *Leo* in 1884 but was in command of the *Calypso* from 1890-1896 and 1902. He died in 1906 aboard SS *Ebro* on her homeward passage just before the ship reached Spurn Head at the mouth of the Humber.

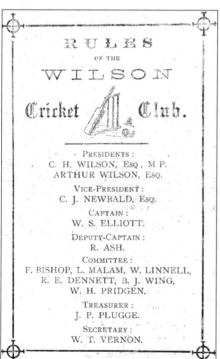

Wilson Cricket Club Team 1886. From left to right (back row); W. King (scorer); C.W. Davy; R.A. Medd; B.G. Newton; J.S. Campion, J.V. Burton, R.Lonsdale (umpire); middle row, R.H. Sawyer, W. Laurillard, R. Ash Jnr (captain); F.R. Bolton and T.H. Lyon; front row B.J. Wing and E.L. Newham. Note the badge of the Wilson line pennant on Wing's shirt.

Rules of the Wilson Cricket Club. Recreational activities were eagerly pursued by the Wilson staff, with football, cricket and hockey to the fore.

Four
Acquisitions
A Shipyard and a Hull
Rival

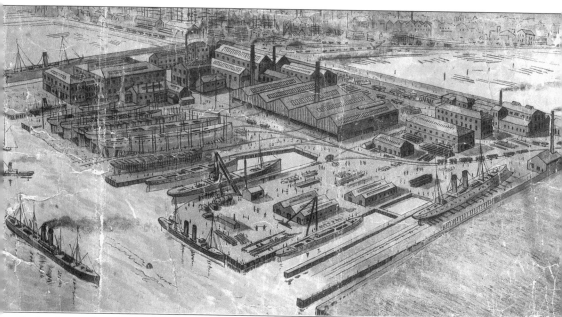

Earles shipyard c.1900. Loss-making naval contracts and a decade of labour problems led to the company being put into liquidation. In 1901, Charles Henry Wilson seized the opportunity to buy the yard for £150,000. Up to that time, the yard had produced no less than ninety-three vessels for the Wilson fleet. The site on the Humber bank was self-contained with its own foundry, engine works, pattern makers, blacksmith and carpenters shops and access by rail to bring in raw materials.

SS *Dago*, built 1902 for Wilsons at Caledon shipyard, Dundee. She was used as a supply ship at Gibraltar during the First World War and after forty years service was sunk by German aircraft while sailing from Lisbon to Oporto with general cargo on 15 March 1942.

BAILEY & LEETHAM,

LIMITED,

HULL, LONDON, NEWCASTLE-ON-TYNE, AND MANCHESTER.

The Fleet consists of

"Argyle."
"Austria."
"Bona."
"Delta."
"Envoy."
"Esperanza."
"Essex."
"Fairy."
"Genoa."
"Jaffa."
"Kotka."
"Lorne."
"Narva."
"Orla."
"Oxford."
"Pera."
"Ronda."
"Sultan."
"Sultana."
"Syria."
"Wm. Bailey."
"Una."
"Zara."

STEAM SHIP OWNERS
AND
GENERAL FORWARDING AGENTS.

Bailey and Leetham, list of sailings 1901. The expansion of the Wilson fleet reached a climax in 1903 with the purchase of Bailey & Leetham, long time rivals in the Baltic trade. These additional twenty-three vessels served St. Petersburg, Konigsberg, Copenhagen, Reval, as well as Hamburg, Venice, Trieste and Palermo.

SS *Sultan*, *c.*1910. Built at Earle's shipyard in 1867 for Gee & Co. of Hull, and purchased in 1881 by Bailey & Leetham. She served Wilson's until 1914 when she was sold to French owners and finally broken up in 1923. She was 216ft (66m) long and 994 tons gross and could carry seventy-two passengers in three classes.

SS *Ronda*, *c.*1910. Built in 1889 by J. Blumer of Sunderland as the *Rydal Holme*, she had an old-fashioned clipper bow and female figurehead. Bought by Bailey & Leetham in 1902 and renamed *Ronda*, she was sold by Wilsons in 1915 to be used as a block ship at Burra Sound, Scapa Flow.

SS *Bona*, *c*.1905. Built in 1883 by Short Bros, Sunderland, as the *Highland Prince* and bought by Bailey & Leetham in 1890. She was renamed *Bona.* Sold by Wilsons to W. Kunstmann, Stettin, in 1905, and fully broken up in 1933.

SS *Una* towed by a paddle-tug, *c*.1905. Built by J. Scott of Kinghorn in 1899 for Bailey & Leetham she was in the Wilson fleet from 1903 to 1909. After sale to a Spanish company she was sunk in 1938 by nationalist aircraft at Palamos during the Spanish Civil War but raised and was in service until 1960.

SS *Ohio*, *c*.1900. Built in 1880 for the Royal Exchange Shipping Company, London, she was purchased in 1887 by Wilsons but sailed under her original name *Egyptian Monarch* until 1893. Renamed *Ohio* she was sold to London owners in 1904 and was wrecked the same year at Ping Yang inlet, Korea, sailing from Muroran to Chinnampho with a cargo of railway sleepers.

SS *Castello*, *c*.1910. She was built for Wilsons in 1896 by William Doxford of Sunderland to their 'turret-ship' design. The hull shape was intended to maximise the amount of cargo for the minimum dues for passage through the Suez Canal. She was 351ft (92m) long and 3,635 tons gross. Sold to Greek owners in 1914, she was sunk by a German submarine in 1916.

SS *Zara*. Built by William Hamilton of Port Glasgow in 1897 for Bailey & Leetham she sailed for Wilsons from 1903 until torpedoed by a German submarine in April 1917 sailing from London to Trondheim with general cargo. Sixteen crew and eleven passengers were lost.

SS *Volo*, September 1899. A postcard of the steamer in Stettin, R.W. Massam, Commander. Built at Earles in 1890, 260ft (107m) long and 1,289 tons gross, she was sold for breaking in 1924.

Caricature of Charles Henry Wilson by Ape in *Vanity Fair* magazine. After the takeover of Bailey & Leetham in 1903, the Wilson Line became the biggest privately owned steamship company in the world. In March 1904, the fleet comprised ninety-nine sea-going vessels and four tugs. The company also owned its own shipyard and had a major stake in Amos & Smith, marine engineers.

Wilson Printing Works, Dock Street. The self-contained nature of Wilsons operation not only included all the obvious maritime trades but also their own printing shop which could turn out advertising material, company ledgers, log books, masters manuals, and all the myriad paper-work involved in running a major commercial enterprise.

Wilson Line Prize Band, 1906. The Wilson band was popular at charitable events in Hull and the region. In 1906, they were winners of the Peoples Challenge Shield at the Crystal Palace.

SS *Ebro*, built 1889 by Richardson, Duck & Co. of Stockton-on-Tees. Wilson masters were no strangers to dramatic rescues on the High Seas but in 1908, one of them was able to make his contribution on the shore. The *Ebro* was tied up at the port of Messina, Sicily on 26 December, when a tidal wave struck, generated by a tremendous earthquake in Calabria, on the toe of Italy.

Crew of the *Ebro*, 1909. The tidal wave devastated the town and *Ebro* herself was lifted bodily against the quayside, damaging the plates all along one side. As soon as the initial shock subsided, Capt. Duffill (middle of front row) organised his crew into shore rescue parties.

Commemorative medal, awarded by the King of Italy to each member of the crew who had saved sixteen adults and three babies from the waterlogged ruins of the town. The vessel was sold four years later to Greek owners and was torpedoed in 1917 sailing from the Tyne to Palermo with a cargo of coal.

SS *Montebello*, *c*.1900. She was built by Richardson, Duck & Co. of Stockton-on-Tees in 1890 with accommodation for sixty-nine first class, twenty second class and some 600 emigrants. She remained in service until 1910 when she was sold to Spanish owners and then scrapped in 1930.

Capt. Colbeck (on the steps) and crew of the steam yacht *Morning*, 1902. While Chief Officer of the *Montebello*, he was asked by the Royal Geographical Society to take the *Morning* with provisions and supplies to aid Captain Scott's *Discovery* expedition.

Colbeck and Robert Falcon Scott (right), 1903. Colbeck found *Discovery* stuck in the ice but she was broken free with charges of gun cotton. Previously Capt. Colbeck had been Chief Navigation Officer with the British Antarctic Expedition of 1898-1900 led by the Norwegian, G.E. Borchgrevink. Scott named Cape Colbeck in his honour.

SS *Aaro*, 1909. Built at Earles shipyard in 1909, 301ft (104m) long and 2,603 tons gross, she was the first Wilson vessel to be fitted with wireless telegraphy. She had accommodation for 104 first class, forty second class and ninety-four third class as well as 502 steerage passengers. She was sunk in the North Sea by U-20 on 1 August, 1916.

RMS *Eskimo*, a twin-screw steamer launched at Earles shipyard in 1910, 331ft (101m) long and 3,326 tons gross. She had accommodation for 109 first class; thirty-nine second class and 420 third class as originally built.

The dining Salon of RMS *Eskimo*. This contemporary postcard shows a restrained, almost austere, elegance.

Salon aboard RMS *Eskimo*, equipped with grand piano. A handsome, powerful (186 nominal horse power from two four-cylinder engines) vessel she was a favourite for the summer cruises along the Norway Coast.

Capt. Bean and a group of VIPs on board RMS *Eskimo*. Note the master's starched white collar, white gloves and well-polished shoes.

SS *Bayardo*, January 1912 was launched at Earles shipyard in 1911. On her thirteenth voyage she ran aground in thick fog on the Middle Sands in the Humber while attempting to enter Alexandra dock. Everyone was taken off safely, and much of the cargo and fittings were salvaged, but she broke her back and was declared a total loss. Fitted with refrigerating machinery she was the biggest vessel in the North Sea trade before 1929.

2nd Edition.

1911

Wilson Line

HULL.

ROYAL MAIL

Passenger & Cargo Services

Thos. Wilson, Sons & Co., Ltd., HULL.

Wilson line, brochure for 1911. The cover features a colour image of the *Eskimo*, the vessel most widely used to advertise the company's services. In 1914-1915, she served as an Armed Merchant Cruiser but after return to trading she was captured while sailing from Oslo to Newcastle. The Germans used her as a net depot ship and, though returned to Wilsons after the war, she was not refitted and was sold to French owners in 1921.

THE ILLUSTRATED LONDON NEWS.

REGISTERED AS A NEWSPAPER FOR TRANSMISSION IN THE UNITED KINGDOM, AND TO CANADA AND NEWFOUNDLAND BY MAGAZINE POST.

No. 3768.– VOL. CXXXIX.   SATURDAY, JULY 8. 1911.   With Supplement in Colours: The Beautiful Scenery of the Russian Ballet.   {SIXPENCE.

The Copyright of all the Editorial Matter, both Engravings and Letterpress, is Strictly Reserved in Great Britain, the Colonies, Europe, and the United States of America.

Hull Dock Strike, 1911. During this dock strike in 1911 stewardesses and other women employees of the Wilson line joined in to help unload a consignment of butter (perishable of course) from the steamer *Titania*. Despite a cordon of police, angry strikers on nearby timber stacks and lighters forced them to stop.

56

Five
Death and War

The funeral cortege of Lord Nunburnholme at Warter Priory, 31 October 1907. After more than thirty years as a Liberal MP, Charles Henry Wilson, chairman of the Wilson Line, was raised to the peerage. Sadly, he died suddenly the following year on 27 October. Led by the clergy, and accompanied by masters and engineers of the Wilson Line, the coffin was laid to rest in the Italian Gardens of his house in the country. Nunburnholme left an estate of £988,386 2s 2d (gross).

Warter Priory was purchased from Lord Muncaster in 1878 by Charles Wilson who was buried in the grounds. The house was expanded from a modest Jacobean structure but was demolished in 1972 and the farmlands are now cultivated as part of a large commercial farming estate.

In 1903 Arthur Wilson finally retired as M.F.H. of the Holderness hunt. The huge fleet formed that year by the take over of Bailey and Leetham must have been as much as the two brothers could handle. He succeeded Charles as chairman but was diagnosed as suffering from stomach cancer in 1908 and he himself died on 21 October 1909 in his seventy third year.

The funeral, 22 October 1909. There was a memorial service in Holy Trinity church, the city's principal place of worship, at the same time as the funeral at Kirkella church. Afterwards the widow and her unmarried daughter Muriel went to winter in the Riviera.

The band of Thomas Wilson, Sons & Co. outside the convalescent home, Whiternsea, East Yorkshire. Kenneth Wilson, Arthur's second son became chairman and the second Lord Nunburnholme, Charles' son, was appointed deputy. Clive Wilson, another of Arthur's sons, and Guy Wilson MP, Charles younger son were also on the board. For a time at least it was business as usual.

The Funeral of Mr. Arthur Wilson.

A Special Train will run from Hull as follows for the conveyance of Members of the Staff who desire to attend the Funeral at Kirkella at 3 o'clo Monday afternoon next the 25th instant :

Cannon Street Station - - dep. 2-15 p.m.

Beverley Road „ - - „ 2-20 „

Willerby - - - - arr. 2-30 „

An Ordinary Train will leave Willerby Station on the return journ 3-56 p.m. and a Special Train at 4-10 p.m. The latter train will wait until a later if it should be necessary.

Tickets can be obtained on application to the Secretary or Marine Superinte

It is proposed to close the Office at Noon on Monday until 5 p.m. to the Members of the Staff to attend either the Funeral at Kirkella or the Memorial S at Holy Trinity Church, Hull.

THOS. WILSON, SONS & CO.

HULL, October 22nd, 1909.

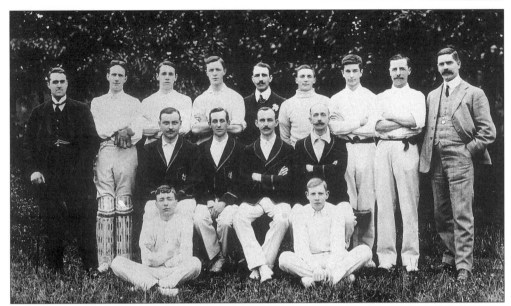

Thomas Wilson & Sons Ltd, Cricket Club. Sports teams were as popular as ever with the Wilson staff and here we have the 1910 cricket team. Back row from left to right; L. Donkin (Hon. Sec.), W. Eckles, B. Brumby, C. Graves, H. Leybourne, A. Elston, F. Illingworth, H. Featherstone, J.M.. Curtis (Hon. Treasurer); middle row G.E. Gibson, F. Lancaster, F. Bird (captain), R. Winn; and front row C. Rockingham and S. Joys.

WEST HULL ELECTION, 1910.

Your VOTE and INTEREST are respectfully solicited on behalf of

GUY WILSON

Printed and Published by " NEWS," Printing Works, Hull.

Guy Greville Wilson, 1910. Charles Henry Wilson had married Florence Wellesley, a great niece of the Duke of Wellington, in 1871. Their eldest son C.H. Wellesley Wilson, known as Tommy, became the second Lord Nunburnholme. Guy the younger son followed in his father's footsteps as Liberal Member of Parliament for West Hull and was first elected in 1907.

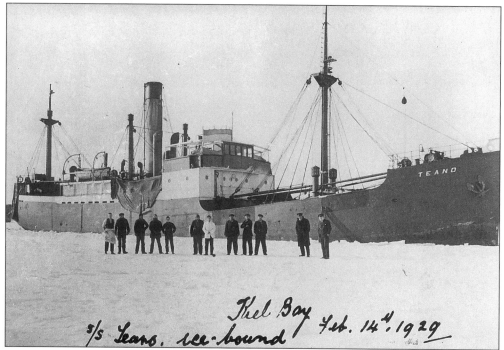

SS *Teano*, icebound in Kiel Bay, 14 February 1929. The Scandinavian and Baltic trade remained a significant part of the Wilson Line's business, so in the winter season there was always the possibility of becoming fast in the ice.

SS *Sappho*; built at Earles shipyard in 1903, was trapped in the ice near Archangel in 1915 and was abandoned on 24 December. Twenty crew perished trying to reach safety and only three survived. All would have fared better by staying on board for the vessel remained afloat in the ice field until May the following year.

Wilson staff marching to the recruiting office at the outbreak of the First World War, more than 100 clerks and other personnel enlisted. The Wilson Line fleet – as indeed were the fleets of all merchant shipping companies – was a vital part of the war effort, braving mines and submarine attacks to bring vital food and essential supplies to Britain.

SS *Borodino*, 1914. Built in 1911 at Earles shipyard, she was used by the Admiralty as a floating shop of the Junior Army and Navy stores Ltd, and was anchored at Scapa Flow for the convenience of the officers of the Grand Fleet. From left to right; Mr Christian (Chief Steward), Mr Baxter (Second Officer), Mr W.J. Allen (Junior Army and Navy Stores), Captain W.J. Norton, Mr A.H. Downing (Junior Army & Navy Stores), Mr Smith (Chief Engineer) and Mr Wass (Second Engineer).

SS *Borodino*, designated as M.F.A. (Merchant Fleet Auxiliary) No.6. There was a comprehensive range of goods, tinned foods, biscuits, poultry and game, tobacco and cigars, etc. for sale. A notice also advertises a hairdressing salon on the main deck, port side, and there was a laundry too.

SS *Castro*. Built in 1911 at Earles shipyard. She was in the Kiel Canal when war was declared and seized by the German authorities. Disguised as the Norwegian vessel *Aud* she was used in an attempt to supply arms to the Irish insurgents. At Tralee Bay, 20 April 1916, the reception party failed to appear and after a chase by the armed trawler *Lord Heneage*, her master, Captain Spindler, scuttled the vessel off Daunt Rock, on the 22 April.

SS *Cito*; built for Wilsons at Earles shipyard in 1899. In 1906 the Wilson and North Eastern Railway Shipping Company was formed in which Wilson's managed vessels for the NER in the services to Antwerp, Ghent, Dunkirk and Hamburg. Initially five steamers *Cito*, *Dynamo*, *Juno*, *Bruno* and *Hero* were purchased by the new company. *Cito* was sunk by torpedo boat destroyers in May 1917, the master and ten of the crew of twenty were killed.

SS *Gourko*. Built at Earles shipyard in 1911 she was refrigerated and used to take supplies of meat to the Grand Fleet at Scapa Flow. She survived until the Second World War and was sunk by a mine off Dunkirk in 1940 where she was intended to be used as a blockship.

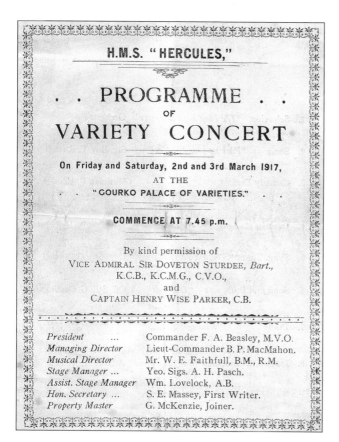

H.M.S. "HERCULES,"

. . PROGRAMME . .

OF

VARIETY CONCERT

On Friday and Saturday, 2nd and 3rd March 1917,

AT THE

. . "GOURKO PALACE OF VARIETIES." . .

COMMENCE AT 7.45 p.m.

By kind permission of

VICE ADMIRAL SIR DOVETON STURDEE, *Bart.*,
K.C.B., K.C.M.G., C.V.O.,
and
CAPTAIN HENRY WISE PARKER, C.B.

President ...	Commander F. A. Beasley, M.V.O.
Managing Director	Lieut-Commander B. P. MacMahon.
Musical Director	Mr. W. E. Faithfull, B.M., R.M.
Stage Manager ...	Yeo. Sigs. A. H. Pasch.
Assist. Stage Manager	Wm. Lovelock, A.B.
Hon. Secretary ...	S. E. Massey, First Writer.
Property Master	G. McKenzie, Joiner.

Programme for the *Gourko*, Palace of Varieties 2-3 March 1917. Between voyages entertainments by and for the serviceman were a mixture of comic sketches and popular songs, including old favourites like 'Pack up your troubles'.

Presentation silver plaque from the officers and men of the Grand Fleet to the SS *Gourko* (Capt. J.R. Owen), the scene of 'seven hundred entertainments witnessed by 300,000 officers and men'.

SS *Calypso*. Launched at Earles shipyard in 1904 she was hired as an armed merchant cruiser and briefly named HMS *Calyx* before returning to Wilsons in 1915 as the *Calypso*. Torpedoed and sunk by U-53 in the Skagerrak with the loss of thirty lives, including the entire crew, while sailing from London to Kristiansand.

SS *Hull*. Launched by Caledon of Dundee in 1907 for Wilson's and North Eastern Railway Shipping Company she was seized in Hamburg at the outbreak of war. In 1916, she was converted into a buoy tender by the Germans, and subsequently returned to Hull. Her crew were among those British merchant seaman interned at Ruhleben, Berlin.

Ruhleben internment camp; barrack twelve. Situated on the outskirts of Berlin near the racecourse; conditions in the camp were spartan but food parcels and letters from home kept up spirits. In 1917-1918, Germany was suffering severe shortages and the diet became even more restricted.

The internees' magazine, Christmas edition 1915. Musical & theatrical entertainments became a staple part of the camp's activities, keeping minds and bodies exercised throughout the long imprisonment. A camp magazine proved extremely popular.

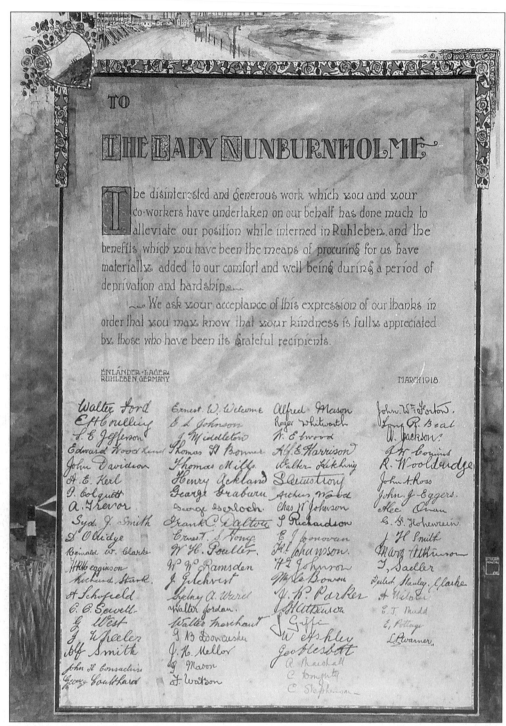

TO

THE LADY NUNBURNHOLME

The disinterested and generous work which you and your co-workers have undertaken on our behalf has done much to alleviate our position while interned in Ruhleben, and the benefits which you have been the means of procuring for us have materially added to our comfort and well being during a period of deprivation and hardship.

We ask your acceptance of this expression of our thanks in order that you may know that your kindness is fully appreciated by those who have been its grateful recipients.

ENLÄNDER·LAGER· RUHLEBEN, GERMANY

MARCH 1918.

Testimonial, 1916. A hand-written and decorated testimonial from all the Wilson Line employees who had been interned in Ruhleben for the duration. Lady Nunburnholme had evidently made great efforts to supply comforts to the internees, seventy-eight of whom signed this token of appreciation.

Six
A New Era

The Wilson offices, c.1920. It may have seemed to the casual observer that with the end of the war, the firm's fortunes would be rebuilt and Wilsons would return to their former glory. The 1920s, however, proved very difficult and the Depression years hit shipping very hard.

Oswald Sanderson (1863-1926), managing director, started his career with Wilsons before joining his father's firm, Sanderson & Co., in the USA, who acted as agents for the Wilson Line among others. Appointed managing clerk in 1891 at a salary of £4,000 a year, he joined the board in 1902 and became managing director in 1905 at £6,000 a year, with a share of the profits.

Painting of Sir John Reeves Ellerman Bt (1862-1933) by Sir Luke Fildes. Antagonism between Sanderson and 'Tommy' Wilson (second Lord Nunburnholme), the heavy war losses (forty-nine out of the pre-war fleet of ninety-two) and the effects on trade of the Russian Revolution resulted in the family's decision to sell the Wilson line to Sir John Ellerman in 1917 for £4.1 million. Ellerman, who was born in Hull, and was the son of a German corn merchant and shipping agent, became chairman.

ROLL OF HONOUR

ELLERMAN'S WILSON LINE LIMITED.

MARINE DEPARTMENT.

Names of Captains, Officers, and Cadets serving in the Company's Steamers who lost their lives at sea during the Great European War.

DATE	SHIP	NAME	RANK	DATE	SHIP	NAME	RANK
Jan. 22nd, 1915	s.s. HYDRO	G. Sharp	Master	May 12th, 1918	s.s. IBIS	F. Cook	Master
Jan. 22nd, 1915	s.s. HYDRO	G. H. Duffill	2nd Officer	May 12th, 1918	s.s. IBIS	R. Matthews	Chief Officer
Dec. 24th, 1915	s.s. SAPPHO	J. Martin	Master	May 12th, 1918	s.s. IBIS	J. W. Day	2nd Officer
Dec. 24th, 1915	s.s. SAPPHO	F. J. Brumby	Chief Officer	May 12th, 1918	s.s. IBIS	J. Robertson	3rd Officer
Feb. 26th, 1916	s.s. DIDO	J. B. Taylor	Master	June 21st, 1916	s.s. MONTEBELLO	G. E. Andrew	Master
Feb. 26th, 1916	s.s. DIDO	J. W. Altoft	2nd Officer	June 21st, 1916	s.s. MONTEBELLO	B. Craven	Chief Officer
Feb. 26th, 1916	s.s. DIDO	E. Vinson	3rd Officer	June 21st, 1916	s.s. MONTEBELLO	B. Friis	2nd Officer
July 9th, 1916	s.s. CALYPSO	O. C. Smith	Master	June 21st, 1916	s.s. MONTEBELLO	W. Spain	3rd Officer
July 9th, 1916	s.s. CALYPSO	H. Joules	Chief Officer	June 21st, 1916	s.s. MONTEBELLO	D. R. King	Cadet
July 9th, 1916	s.s. CALYPSO	T. Stockdale	2nd Officer	June 21st, 1916	s.s. MONTEBELLO	J. B. Senior	Cadet
Nov. 16th, 1916	s.s. VASCO	W. Donaldson	Master	July 8th, 1916	s.s. CHICAGO	G. W. Margerison	3rd Officer
April 12th, 1917	s.s. TORO	D. M. Tether	2nd Officer	Aug 6th, 1918	s.s. BIRUTA	W. B. Seniscal	Master
April 12th, 1917	s.s. TORO	E. Moorhouse	Cadet	Dec. 23rd, 1918	s.s. GITANO	W. J. Decent	Master
April 13th, 1917	s.s. ZARA	W. M. Golightly	Chief Officer	Dec. 23rd, 1918	s.s. GITANO	J. W. Barron	Chief Officer
May 17th, 1917	s.s. CITO	G. W. Orme	Master	Dec. 23rd, 1918	s.s. GITANO	J. J. Glenton	2nd Officer
May 17th, 1917	s.s. CITO	M. W. M. Donovan	2nd Officer	Dec. 23rd, 1918	s.s. GITANO	J. R. Simpkins	Cadet
May 20th, 1917	s.s. TYCHO	G. B. Williams	Master	Dec. 23rd, 1918	s.s. GITANO	G. G. Barnes	Cadet
May 20th, 1917	s.s. TYCHO	E. Carmichael	2nd Officer				
Feb. 1st, 1918	s.s. CAVALLO	R. A. D. Gardham	2nd Officer				
Feb. 1st, 1918	s.s. CAVALLO	O. H. Thomson	Cadet				
Feb. 12th, 1918	s.s. POLO	C. A. C. Clarke	Cadet				
Feb. 20th, 1918	s.s. HARROGATE	F. B. Boyle	Master				
Mar. 3rd, 1918	s.s. ROMEO	J. Neale	Master				
Mar. 3rd, 1918	s.s. ROMEO	A. Pitts	Chief Officer				
Mar. 3rd, 1918	s.s. ROMEO	H. L. Pardoe	2nd Officer				
April 30th, 1918	s.s. UMBA	J. W. Young	Master				
April 30th, 1918	s.s. UMBA	R. Hodgson	Chief Officer				
April 30th, 1918	s.s. UMBA	T. W. Kerridge	2nd Officer				

for King & Country

Roll of Honour of Ellerman's Wilson Line captains, officers and cadets who lost their lives in the Great War. Forty-six names are listed and this was aside from seamen and passengers who had been killed. The last vessel to be registered under the ownership of Thomas Wilson Sons & Co. was the *Oswego*, sunk by U-86 in May 1917.

ELLERMAN'S WILSON LINE
PRINTING WORKS.

Manifest Forms.   Visiting and Business Cards.
Bills of Lading.   Tally Books.
Sailing Cards.   Log Books.
Letter Headings and Memo. Forms.   Record Books.
Invoice and Statement Forms.   Company Notices.
Loose Leaf Forms and Binders.   Calendars.
Inter-Office Forms.   Booklets, illustrated in line or half
Envelopes, all kinds.   tone, etc., etc.

All classes of color work.

The Book-binding Dept. is fully equipped for the manufacture of
bound Books of all kinds, Ledgers, Cash Books and Day Books. Statistical
and other columnar Books involving intricate ruling.

Sundry Office Stationery, such as

Pens.   Inks.   Pen and Pencil Carbons.
Pencils.   Erasers.   Typewriter Carbons & Ribbons.
Paper Fasteners.   Memo. Books.   Shorthand Note Books.
Letter Copying Books.   Indexed Books, etc., etc.

We have special terms with all the principal typewriter Companies
and Machines of any make can be supplied at considerable reductions on
published rates.

The Company is registered as a member of the Master Printers
Federation and all work carried out is on the general and recognised
terms of labour applicable to all manufacturing Printers.

Ellerman's Wilson Line, Printing Works. The self-sufficiency of the old family firm continued under the new ownership. The printing works not only supplied the Wilson Line but offered a comprehensive range of products to customers at large.

WILSON LINE.

NOTICE TO PASSENGERS.

Boat Assembly Stations.

In cases of Emergency on hearing the General Emergency Signal, viz. :

SEVEN SHORT BLASTS followed by ONE LONG BLAST,

Passengers must put on their Life Jackets which will be found in racks at the top of each Cabin, secure warm clothing and proceed to the Assembly Stations as quickly as possible in a quiet and orderly manner, in order to prevent as much as possible disorder or panic and take instructions from the responsible Officers in attendance there.

The nature and meaning of the General Emergency Signal, is not to be taken as a signal for the abandonment of the ship, but is intended to secure the orderly marshalling of passengers to the appointed Assembly Station, in order that they may be readily drafted from them to the required positions on the Embarkation Deck, as circumstances may necessitate, should the occurrence of a serious accident make this advisable.

Emergency Notice. The printing works not only supplied ledgers, letterheads, log books, etc., but all the sundry notices for ship and shore, like this instruction for passengers in case of emergency.

Muriel Thetis Wilson (1875-1964) painted by Sir William Blake Richmond RA, 1895. The oyster satin gown was made by Madame Clapham, a noted Hull dressmaker who also regularly made clothes for Queen Maude of Norway, thanks to the influence of the Wilson family. Muriel was a frequent guest of the Duke and Duchess of Devonshire at Chatsworth and was in great demand for amateur theatricals.

Charity performance for the Soldier's and Sailor's Families Association held at the Palace Theatre, Hull, by Mrs Arthur Wilson. The casts for such events included members of the family and professionals such as Mrs Beerbohm Tree and Eillie Norwood, now best remembered for his characterisation of Sherlock Holmes in no less than forty-seven silent films between 1921 and 1923.

Muriel Wilson as the Muse of History. There were numerous theatricals at Tranby Croft, the family home of Arthur and Mary Wilson. Historical pageants and poses of allegorical characters were a popular feature of Edwardian entertainments.

'Patience', 30/31 January, 2/3 February 1882 – this performance at Tranby Croft was by kind permission of W.S. Gilbert and Arthur Sullivan; the first public performance had been on 23 April 1881, less than a year before.

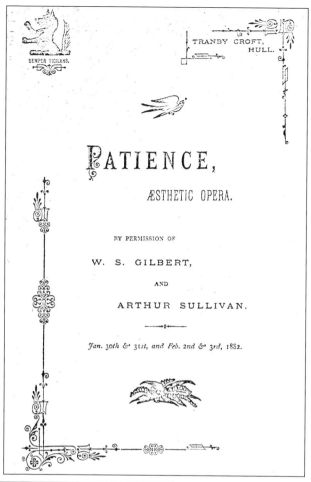

The cast of 'Patience'. The performers are chiefly friends and visitors, Ethel Wilson, Arthur and Mary's second daughter, plays the title role. She later married Edward Lycett Green. Note that Arthur Wilson is credited as one of the directors of the show!

Sketch of Muriel Wilson by John Singer Sargent, the noted painter of society portraits. A visitor to Tranby Croft and a frequent contact in London (where the family had a town house in Grosvenor Place) was Winston Churchill. His offer of marriage in 1904 was rejected and he says in a letter 'you dwell apart – as lofty as shining and alas as cold as a snow-clad peak'. She is also reported to have broken off engagements to the Duke of Marlborough and Lord Willoughby d'Eresby.

The marriage of Muriel Wilson, 1 September 1917. Here her brother Clive, a veteran of the Boer war where he gained the DSO poses with two of the bridesmaids. The marriage was at Anlaby Church, about a mile from Tranby Croft, to Captain Richard Edward Warde M.C., nine years her junior, who tragically died in a car accident in 1932.

Villa Maryland at Cap Ferrat on the French Riviera. As well as Tranby Croft, and a London home in the metropolis, Arthur also acquired this villa, which was named after his wife. It was a favourite resort of both Mary and her youngest daughter Muriel where she could meet with her society friends and enjoy the mild Mediterranean winters.

Arthur Stanley 'Jack' Wilson (1868-1938) at the races. After the sale of the family business, it was left largely in the capable hands of Oswald Sanderson and the huge windfall enabled the children of Arthur and Charles Henry Wilson to enjoy life in society and running their country estates. Unionist MP for Holderness he married Alice Filmer daughter of Sir Edmund Filmer Bt of Sutton Park, Kent.

SS *Arctic Prince* in Hull docks *c.*1926. Wilsons tried to make the best use of their vessels and experienced seamen in very bad trading conditions. The Hull fishing firm of Hellyers embarked on a scheme for catching halibut off Greenland, line-fishing from dories carried abroad a mother ship. The *Arctic Prince* was commanded and crewed by Wilson personnel.

Ellerman's Wilson Officers of the *Arctic Queen* which entered service in the halibut fishing in 1928; Captain Phillips is third from left. The enterprise was a joint venture between Hellyers and Engvald Baldersheim of Bergen, Norway.

SS *Borodino* 1932. In June that year the *Borodino* rendezvoused with the *Arctic Prince* to take on board a consignment of fish. On board the Wilson vessel were a German camera crew which had been shooting a film entitled *SOS Iceberg*.

Cameramen of the Universal-Fanck Greenland Film expedition aboard the *Borodino*. A polar bear borrowed from a German zoo was taken to Greenland by the company as it was uncertain whether a wild one would be discovered when required and its behaviour would have been altogether unpredictable.

Ernest Udet (1896-1941), the leading German flying ace of the First World War. He was in charge of the flying sequences which featured in the film. From 1935 he was in the German air ministry but, disillusioned by the Nazi regime, committed suicide by crashing his aircraft.

Leni Reifenstahl (1902-); the star of the film. Soon afterwards she set up her own film-making unit making documentaries for the Nazi party, notably *Triumph of the Will* (1935) and *Olympia*, the film of the 1936 Olympics. Though propagandising, her work showed great artistry. Post-war she worked as a photo-journalist.

Earles crane in Kowloon, 1988. Though Ellermans ordered ten vessels for various constituent companies from the yard between 1917 and 1927 the Depression years spelled the end. Hull's biggest shipyard was totally dismantled and all visible traces removed. The great 100 ton tower crane erected by Applebys of Leicester in 1909 was sold and re-erected at Kowloon where it survived the Japanese invasion.

SS *Selby*. Launched at Aberdeen in 1922 for the Wilson and North Eastern Railway Shipping Company. She was transferred to Associated Humber Lines in 1935 and remained in service till 1958. AHL, also managed by Wilsons, was a grouping of Goole Steam Shipping Co. (LMS Railway) Hull and Netherlands Steamship Company and the W.N.E.R.S Co. along with the LNER continental services at Grimsby.

The Wilson Clerks Angling Association. Social activities among Ellerman's Wilson personnel continued to expand and as well as the 'contemplative man's recreation', football, cricket, etc., the more cerebral delights of whist and bridge were available.

Ellerman's Wilson Ladies Hockey Team, c.1930. Since the First World War women had increasingly made their presence felt in commerce and industry. The ladies hockey team sport the Ellerman's Wilson insignia, the blue pennant with J.R.E. initials, above the Wilson pennant, white with a red ball.

Summer Cruises 1935. Offering a high standard of accommodation to passengers, the delights of cruising the Norway Coast helped to maintain income though competition for cargo kept freight rates low. Norwegian cruises were popularised by King Oscar II who, after his coronation in 1873, undertook a journey to the North Cape and the 'Land of the Midnight Sun'.

SS *City of Nagpur*, 1938. Vessels were occasionally swapped between various elements of the Ellerman shipping empire. The *City of Nagpur* became a regular for summer cruises to Norway. This classic image of a vessel steaming through a fjord was a design by Harry Hudson Rodmell, the noted marine artist, which was used as a poster as well as on this brochure.

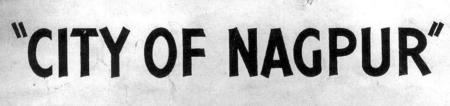

"CITY OF NAGPUR"

MARCH

Composed & Arranged
by
CERES HARPER

Price
1/.

Published by
ARTHUR B. ROBINSON
28 King Street,
BRIDLINGTON.

City of Nagpur, March; sheet music of a March especially written for the *City of Nagpur* by Ceres Harper, a popular local bandleader of the 1930s.

Embarkation Notice, 1939; the illustration shows the very comfortable furnishings of the lounge aboard the *City of Nagpur* which was sailing on summer cruises to Norway virtually until the outbreak of war. The final cruise scheduled for September 1939 was cancelled.

Miss L. James

R.M.S. "CITY OF NAGPUR"

THE LOUNGE

CRUISING FROM HULL, SATURDAY, 29TH JULY, 1939.

EMBARKATION NOTICE.

ELLERMAN'S WILSON LINE, LIMITED,
PASSENGER OFFICE,
HULL.

WILSON LINE
CRUISING STAKES.

Held under the DOGGER BANK JOCKEY CLUB RULES.

RACE CARD.

"Well Run"

CRUISES 1939.

THE COURSE:
Somewhere between Spurn Light Vessel and Oslo Fjord.

On Board R.M.S. "CITY OF NAGPUR."

ELLERMAN'S WILSON LINE, LIMITED,
HULL.

Race Card, 1939. Like the great ocean-going passenger liners those aboard even the short distance cruise vessels enjoyed a whole range of entertainments including dances, fancy dress, deck games and sweepstakes.

WILSON LINE, HULL.

JERSEY NEW POTATO SEASON, 1939.

DEAR SIRS,
        We beg to inform you that we are arranging to run our usual service of fast steamers between

JERSEY and HULL

(weather and other circumstances permitting) **during the New Potato Season, 1939.**

During the height of the Season steamers are intended to leave **JERSEY** for **HULL** **on Mondays, Tuesdays, Wednesdays and Saturdays.**

Special attention is directed to the fact that discharge of Potatoes shipped from Jersey on Saturday is commenced at 6 a.m. on Monday.

These steamers will discharge at the **RIVERSIDE QUAY, HULL,** and as they can berth at any state of the tide, quick despatch is assured.

With this reliable service to Hull, and the special arrangements made by us with the Railway Companies, the Hull route offers exceptional facilities for the rapid transit of the potato traffic to the various inland towns and markets.

The goods are carried subject to the conditions of the Jersey printed form of receipt, and the conditions set forth in this circular, also to the conditions and/or regulations of any Railway Company by whom the goods may be conveyed.

The **HULL** steamers will load as usual at the **ALBERT PIER, JERSEY.**

We hereby give notice that we cannot accept responsibility for the following:—
        Delay in loading or unloading or detention of steamers at Jersey or Hull.
        Delay in the journey of the steamer or suspension of sailings.
        Delay to traffic on English railways.
        Delay on Quay at Hull, or in despatch therefrom owing to Strikes, Railway Restrictions, or other causes.

NOTE. The Rate of Freight from JERSEY to HULL will be 32/- per ton. This Rate does not include Insurance.

For Potatoes delivered by us to Motor Vehicles for forwarding to Inland destinations, a charge of **2/-** per ton will be made to cover additional cost of labourage.

Merchants desirous of collecting their Potatoes at Hull by Motor Transport are requested to instruct their Shippers to label the packages **HULL,** in order that same can be kept separate from rail traffic on discharge from steamer, **and also to indicate on consignment notes that forwarding from Hull will take place by Motor vehicle.**

Jersey New Potato Season, 1939. Collecting the annual harvest of new potatoes from Jersey was a regular part of the Wilson line's business. This announcement was for what turned out to be the last consignment before the outbreak of the Second World War.

SS *Accrington*. As in the First World War, many vessels were lost due to mines, submarines and also air attack. During the Second World War the fleet had in fact reduced to a mere nine. The A.H.L. vessels, *Bury, Accrington, Dewsbury, Stockport* and *Melrose Abbey* were used as rescue ships for the Atlantic convoys.

The *Hopewell* motor gun boat. Selected Wilson officers and men were used to man a squadron of five high-powered craft for dashes across the North Sea to neutral Sweden. The master of the *Hopewell*, without hat, is Capt. David 'Ginger' Stokes.

Blockade Buster, 1943. Testing the Oerlikons aboard *Master Standfast*, one of the 'Grey ladies' as the German, called them. They relied mainly on their speed to avoid E boats, coastal batteries and air attack in the narrows of the Kattegat en route between the Humber and Lysekil in Sweden to pick up ball-bearings and strategic metals.

SEAMAN'S RE CORD BOOK

AN D

CERTIFICATES OF DISCHARGE

Official replacement in continuation of Discharge Book No. 1020537

NATIONAL INSURANCE NUMBER
LW/44/72/51/A

UNION OR SOCIETY
Name N.U.S.
No. 593243.

INCOME TAX CODE NUMBER AND DATE

PENSION FUND AND REGISTERED No.

DECLARATION.
I DECLARE (i) that the person to whom this Discharge Book relates has satisfied me that he (she) is a seaman and (ii) that the photograph affixed bearing my official stamp is a true likeness of that person, that the signature within is his (her) true signature, that he (she) possesses the physical characteristics entered within and has stated to me the date and place of his (her) birth as entered within.

SIGNATURE OF SUPT. AT MERCANTILE MARINE OFFICE—

DATE 31 JUL 1952

L. KOHLER 1020537.

M.M.O. EMBOSSING STAMP

NAME OF SEAMAN.
SURNAME (in Block Letters) KOHLER
CHRISTIAN NAMES (in full) Laurence

DATE AND PLACE OF BIRTH 30.7.01 Hull
NATIONALITY British

Height 5'6"
Colour of Eyes Blue
Hair Brown
Complexion Fresh

Tattoo or other Distinguishing Marks Tattooed on right forearm

GRADE NUMBER AND DATE OF ISSUE OF CERTIFICATES OF COMPETENCY HELD

B.S.I.C. Serial No. BS. 145653.

SIGNATURE OF SEAMAN L Kohler

Discharge Book of Lawrie Kohler, one of the crew of the *Gay Corsair*, blockade-runner. Of German descent he had found it impossible to join the Royal Navy in 1914 but in the Second World War was recruited for the dangerous and vital work to maintain supplies of ball-bearings essential to so many machines needed for the war effort.

BUSTERS ALL, FROM THE GALLANT GAY CORSAIR

The crew of *Gay Corsair*; on the right is Bob Tanton, OBE, master; the left hand photograph shows from left to right, F. Clark, Bob Tanton, First Officer Kenneth H. McNeil, Kenneth Park, Lawrence Kohler (bosun) and J. Bird. Lawrie Kohler was invested with the British Empire Medal on 16 May 1944.

Seven
Rebuilding the Fleet

Twin screw ship *Sacramento*, launched at Birkenhead by Cammell Laird in 1945, 434ft (132m) long and 7,096 tons gross is seen here on the Mersey after fitting out. War losses reduced the fleet from thirty-five to a mere nine and a major rebuilding programme was initiated by H.S. Holden, who had been chairman since 1933 when Sir John Ellerman died.

Diploma signed by the secretary of the State of California and presented to Ellerman's Wilson Line in appreciation of their having named the new addition to the post-war fleet after the principal city, Sacramento.

SS *Tasso* built by Swan Hunter at Walker-on-Tyne is here seen leaving the Tyne on her trials on 26 September 1945. By 1946 when H.S. Holden died, nine new vessels had been launched for Wilsons and J.W. Bayley took over as the new chairman. He had overseen the building of a further twelve ships by the time of his death in 1950.

SS *Leo*, another product of the Swan Hunter yard, is seen here while passing under a bridge on the Kiel Canal. After the war most Wilson vessels carried no more than twelve passengers, the maximum number allowable without having to meet the requirements of a passenger certificate. Accommodation was however invariably comfortable with excellent service.

SS *Domino*. Launched in 1947 by Ailsa Shipbuilding Co. of Troon, Ayrshire, she was a modest 296ft (90m) long and 2,302 tons gross. She was fitted with a three-cylinder engine and low pressure turbine with double reduction gearing and hydraulic coupling to the screw shaft, developing 1,625 horse power.

SS *Domino* at Venice *c*.1955. In 1961, she was the last vessel to sail in the American trade for Wilsons, and the following year was sold to African Coasters of Durban. In 1960 Ellerman Wilson Line was operating services from Hull, London, Liverpool, Manchester, Middlesbrough, Newcastle, Aberdeen, Swansea, Newport, Antwerp, Dunkirk among others, to and from Norway, Sweden, Denmark, the Baltic States, Poland, Portugal the Mediterranean, Adriatic and the Levant, Egypt, India, Pakistan, Canada and the USA and the Great Lake ports.

SS *Presto*; a tug launched by Cochrane and Sons Ltd of Selby in 1943 for the Ministry of War Transport as *Empire Sara*. She was purchased in 1946 by Ellerman Wilson Line for £22,500. Along with *Forto* she remained in service until 1968.

Wilson Line lighters. Along with tugs, Wilsons retained their fleet of barges and lighters, maintaining the tradition of self-sufficiency. This is a scene in Albert Dock, Hull, in 1968 with three vessels of the Polish Ocean Lines of Gdynia; from left to right, *Wolin*, *Jaslo* and *Koszalin*.

SS *Rialto*; launched by Swan Hunter on the Tyne on 2 September 1948 as yard number 1860. In February 1966 she was damaged by a freak wave when sailing from St John, New Brunswick, to Aberdeen, and part of the bridge was torn away.

Launch party of SS *Rialto*, on 2 September 1948. The vessel was 401ft (122m) long, 5,005 tons gross and was fitted with a low-pressure turbine, refrigerating machinery and accommodation for twelve passengers. *Rialto* was sold to Cypriot owners in 1970.

SS *Vasco* was built in 1939 and she survived two aerial attacks in 1941. Seen here sunk at Haile Sand on the Humber in December 1948, she was refloated and repaired but was damaged in a collision on the Thames in 1956. *Vasco* was sold to German owners in 1963 after an eventful twenty-four years of service with Wilsons.

SS *Bravo* in Albert Dock, Hull receiving an eighty-three ton roll of steel from a heavy-lift floating crane barge. She features in *Berth 24*, one of the first British Transport Films, made in 1949, which records her arrival from Gothenburg into Alexandra Dock. It is an important record of traditional cargo-handling by teams of stevedores before the advent of containerisation. The film was premiered simultaneously at the Dorchester Theatre, Hull, and the Empire, Leicester Square on 19 May 1950.

A London transport bus being lifted from a Wilson vessel by a forty ton crane to form part of the 1951 Festival of Britain celebrations. Note the pit props on the dock side and the (now demolished) landmark, the clock tower visible bebeath the bus, which overlooked Albert Dock and the Riverside Quay.

SS *Borodino*; launched by Ailsa Shipbuilding Co. of Troon in 1950, she was 295ft (90m) long and 3,206 tons gross, an oil fired steamer. Fitted with refrigerating machinery she was used on regular runs to Copenhagen for consignments of butter and bacon.

SS *Borodino* discharging Danish produce at the Riverside Quay of Hull, 9 November 1959. The 'butter' boats had grey hulls unlike the remainder of the fleet, which were painted dark green – the traditional Wilson colour. The latter, along with the red and black funnel, resulted in the nickname of 'parrot-ships'.

SS *Borodino*; handsomely appointed, she had accommodation for thirty-six first class and twenty third class passengers.

SS *Borodino*; the 'contemporary' decor included a marquetry image of the vessel fronting the bar.

Main staircase of SS *Borodino* under construction. Veneers of walnut, figured sycamore, maple and willow, as well as cherry, obeche, burr oak, padauk and satinwood were all used on the finished structure, built by Armstrongs of Hull.

SS *Borodino* was chosen to represent Ellerman's Wilson Line at the Coronation Spithead Review on 15 June. Here she is decked with lights and sporting an illuminated E II R sign behind the funnel.

SS *Borodino* arrived at Spithead, spick and span, under the command of Captain Ford accompanied by two other Hull vessels, *Loch Torridon*, pioneer of the all year round Greenland fishing, and the *Magrix*. The climax of the festivities was a wonderful firework display with every vessel lit from stem to stern.

Lounge of MV *Cavallo*; launched in 1951 and built by Henry Robb of Leith. She was 296ft (90m) long and 2,340 tons gross. She was the first motor vessel built for Ellerman's Wilson Line and had a high standard of accommodation for her twelve passengers. Note painting of the vessel over the very domestic looking fireplace, complete with vase of flowers.

SS *Aire*; part of the Associated Humber Lines fleet, managed by Ellerman's Wilson Lines, in Humber Dock, Hull on 18 February 1953. Built in 1931 (1,116 tons gross), two other vessels of the fleet are moored immediately behind her, the *Melrose Abbey*, built in 1929 and the *Bury*, a veteran launched in 1911.

SS *Melrose Abbey*; built in 1929 for the Hull & Netherland Steamship Co., one of the last vessels to be launched from Earles shipyard. Taken into the A.H.L. fleet in 1935 and, after nationalisation of the railway companies in 1948, the fleet was jointly owned by the British Transport Commission and Ellerman's Wilson Line.

MV *Bolton Abbey*, built in 1958 by Brooke Marine of Lowestoft for the cargo-passenger trade between Hull and Rotterdam. She was 302ft (92m) long and 2,740 tons gross and could achieve $15\frac{1}{2}$ knots with her Ruston & Hornsby diesel engines. In 1959 she was the first vessel to berth at the Riverside Quay, reconstructed after wartime damage.

MV *Melrose Abbey*; sister ship of *Bolton Abbey*. She was built in 1959 and replaced the old steamer of the same name, making a total of nine vessels in the fleet. A.H.L. used the funnel colours of the old LMS fleet, buff with a black top but separated by a broad red band and the initials in large raised letters painted black.

Fountains Abbey, another of the A.H.L. fleet, built in 1954 at Aberdeen, caught fire in the North Sea, 11 February 1962, with the loss of two of her twenty-two crew. After towing to Amsterdam she was scrapped and temporarily replaced on the Goole-Hamburg run by the *Rijsbergen*.

SS *Cicero*, passing under Tower Bridge, London. Launched by Henry Robb of Leith in 1954 she and the *Rollo* were the last steamers sailing with Ellerman's Wilson Line when they were sold in 1970.

SS *Cicero*; carrying only twelve passengers who were treated to luxury accommodation. This single cabin is spacious and furnished in a modern style using quality hardwood.

SS *Cicero*; the dining room was also very comfortable, with leather upholstered chairs, and crockery and cutlery monogrammed with the company's initials. The scale remains domestic and intimate and Wilson ships were greatly appreciated by the discerning traveller.

The lounge of SS *Cicero*; this also captures the domestic and friendly atmosphere. Note the painting of the vessel over the fireplace. She served for sixteen years in the fleet, mainly in the Gothenburg run before being sold to the Maldives Shipping Co. in 1970.

Trade exhibition held at Naples in 1954, the Mostra d'Oltremare in which Ellerman Lines advertised their Papayanni, and Wilson Line services. On the left is a model of the *Cavallo*. The ship was sold in 1971 along with *Trentino* to the Maldives Shipping Co.

WILSON LINE

HULL
TO
PIRÆUS, THESSALONIKI (Salonica), IZMIR & ISTANBUL

s.s. RINALDO

will receive general cargo up to

FRIDAY, 4th NOVEMBER, 1955

at

No. 31 SHED, ALEXANDRA DOCK

Terms and conditions as specified in List of Sailings Booklet accompanying this announcement

ELLERMAN'S WILSON LINE, LIMITED, HULL

Sailing card for the *Rinaldo* 1955. She was built by William Gray of Hartlepool in 1946 and sold to Greek owners in 1967. J.R. Fewlass had succeeded as chairman in 1950 and after his death in 1959 Ellerman's Wilson Line joined the other fleets in the Ellerman's group under the chairmanship of A.F. Hull; Col G.W. Bayley was managing director at Hull.

The SS *Volo* was built by Swan Hunter on the Tyne in 1946, 284ft (87m) long and 1,797 tons gross. Here she is seen during her commissioning trials. In October 1954, she ran aground at Halden sustaining considerable bottom damage while sailing from Oslo to Hull.

SS *Volo* at Stockholm, 4 November 1960. Wood wool in number two hold caught fire and the blaze took twenty-four hours to bring under control. Much of the ship's superstructure was gutted.

SS *Volo*, 5 November 1960; the fire was still getting worse and the Swedish firemen were all equipped with breathing apparatus to get near the seat of the blaze.

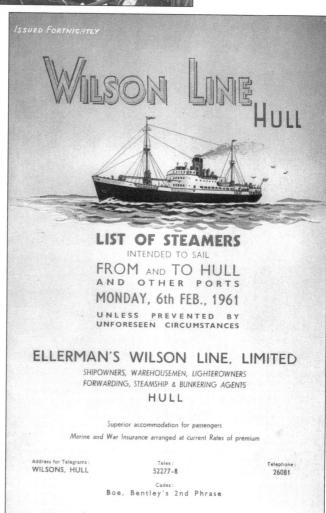

Wilson Line, list of services sailing on 6 February 1961.

SS *Volo* 7 November 1960. Salvaged cargo has been transferred to lighters alongside and the vessel pumped out. She was repaired at Gothenburg and returned to service but was sold to Maltese owners in 1969.

Eight

S-Ships, Spero and Farewell to the Wilson Line

MV *Salerno* in Lisbon; built by Henry Robb of Leith in 1965 she was the first of five vessels, all with names beginning with the initial S, hence the S-class. Wilsons were determined to develop a modern fleet equipped for rapid and efficient cargo-handling.

Launch of MV *Salerno* at Leith on 27 August 1965; she had a chequered career – breaking the inner dock gates of Horten Verft causing damage amounting to two million Norwegian kronor. In 1970 she damaged her rudder on rocks in the Stockholm archipelago and was transferred to Ellerman City Lines in 1973; renamed *City of Corinth*.

MV *Salerno* in the Kiel Canal in 1965 under the command of Capt. G.G. Needham. The on-board cranes allowed the handling of general and containerised or palletised cargo as well as refrigerated containers. There were side-loading doors port and starboard for driving cargo straight into the tween decks. A bow thruster facilitated berthing and docking.

Bridge of MV *Salerno* 1965. Modern and spacious though it is, there are still the traditional steering wheel and telegraph systems, all of which have now vanished in the present-day computerised vessel.

MV *Salmo* was launched by Henry Robb at Leith in 1967 and she was the second of the class to enter service. Here seen at Valetta, Malta, with various British warships in the background. She was transferred to Ellerman City Lines in 1974 and renamed *City of Athens*.

MV *Sorrento* making her maiden voyage, carrying export cargo to Sweden in the Hull/East Sweden service run jointly by Wilson Line and Svea Line of Stockholm. She was transferred to Ellerman City Line in 1974 and renamed *City of Sparta*.

MV *Sangro* was the fifth and last of the S-class built by Henry Robb for Ellerman's Wilson Line Scandinavian and Mediterranean trades. *Salmo*, *Sorrento*, *Silvio* and *Sangro* were all slightly larger than *Salerno*, 308ft (94m) and 1,523 tons gross.

MV *Spero* launched at Cammell Laird, Birkenhead by Mrs G.W. Bayley, wife of the managing director, on 5 May 1966. *Spero* was built as the result of the formation of a consortium of the Svea Line, Swedish Lloyd and Ellerman's Wilson to provide frequent cargo-passenger sailings between Hull-Gothenburg and London-Gothenburg.

MV *Spero*, 454ft (138m) long, 6,916 tons gross and furnished with four Mirrlees oil engines arranged in pairs with each pair coupled to one screw shaft. She made her maiden voyage from Hull to Gothenburg on 31 August 1966.

MV *Spero*; a very impressive, spacious, bridge, with chart table, radar and all modern navigational aids. The aim was to reach a weekly quota of over 3,500 passengers, nearly 1,000 cars and some 10,000 tons of cargo.

Captain David Alexander ('Ginger') Stokes, a Wilson veteran. He joined as a cadet in 1921, was a hero of the 'ball-bearing' run to Sweden during the Second World War, and was chosen to be the master of the *Spero* – E.W.L.'s most expensive vessel ever, built at a cost of some £2 million. He shared command with Capt. Frederick Briggs who took over after Stokes' retirement in the autumn of 1967.

MV *Spero*; in February 1967 the traditional green hull of the Wilson fleet was changed to light grey with white superstructure so as to more closely resemble the white-hulled *Svea* and *Saga*. The three vessels of the consortium had all the appearance of cruise liners.

The new vessel at King George Dock, Hull in 1967. Cars and containers on flats entered at the stern doors; the new roll-on, roll-off vessels needed different dockside facilities from traditional cargo vessels so new terminals were built at Hull, London and Gothenburg for the service.

MV *Spero* leaving King George Dock, Hull aided by a tug. She only just fitted the narrow lock pit entrance from the river Humber.

Sauna bath on MV *Spero*. The whole idea of 'one-class' luxury travel was heavily promoted, facilities were available to all passengers, a maximum of 408, who could enjoy the normal ferry service or a mini-cruise.

A four-berth, family cabin aboard the *Spero*. In addition to maintaining regular passenger schedules, 'mini-cruises' were introduced in the spring of 1967 and were repeated again in the autumn.

Dining room, MV *Spero*. Note the menu card shaped like funnels, bearing the traditional Wilson colours of red with a black top.

Kitchen of MV *Spero*. Having to cater for over 400 passengers, the old style kitchens of Wilson vessels, much more of a domestic scale, were replaced by highly automated and 'industrialised' equipment.

M.V. "Spero"
ELLERMAN'S WILSON LINE LIMITED
3 Z.2.S Crypto Rotapan Cookers
Crypto "Cutomatic" Slicer
EB. 3020 Crypto Mixer
F. 2 Crypto Pommes Frites Slicer
C. 56 Crypto Peeler
Photograph No. SM 2283.

Stewardesses aboard MV *Spero*. There was a conscious attempt to provide the highest quality travel in the most modern way. Decor was a major consideration throughout and the stewardesses all wore specially commissioned two-piece woollen suits which were featured in the *Woman and Home* magazine.

TV lounge of MV *Spero*. A special lounge was set-aside for viewing as befitted the 'age of television'.

Cafeteria, MV *Spero*. For informal meals in daytime the emphasis was on a crisp, clean and efficient cafeteria seating.

Cars, caravans and cargo on flats, waiting to be loaded onto MV *Spero*. The headroom in the cargo area was not sufficient for lorries with containers to drive directly on and off and instead they had to be transferred to trailers or palettes; this reduced efficiency and increased loading times.

J.R. Fewlass jnr, since 1969 deputy manager of E.W.L., Arthur Lowe and Capt. Etches on board *Spero* April 1972. Failing to make an economic return *Spero* was withdrawn from the Gothenburg service and inaugurated a Hull-Zeebrugge ro-ro service. Passengers were again offered mini-cruises (starting at £13.50) aboard this well appointed vessel with the attractions of Bruges and easy access to Holland and France as added incentives.

Arthur Lowe in Brussels, receiving the offerings of the Mannekin-Pis in his top hat, he and the statue both dressed as John Bull. Achieving fame as Leonard Swindley, the shop keeper in Coronation Street, and immortality as Captain Mainwaring in *Dads Army* he was an appropriate choice to launch the new service since his son was a cadet officer with Ellermans.

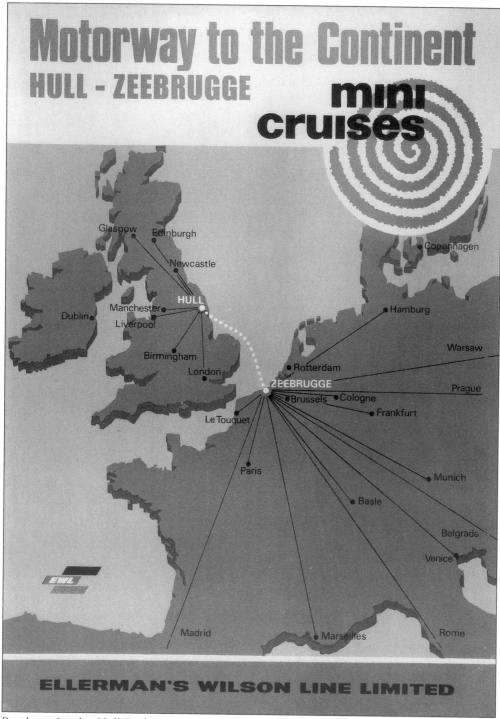

Brochure for the Hull-Zeebrugge mini-cruises, emphasising the easy access to the whole of continental Europe from Zeebrugge.

Humber Airways Limited (H.A.L). The spirit of enterprise which so characterised the company in the late 1960s was emphasised with the extension into air-travel. In 1968 a Grimsby-based air-taxi service was purchased and placed under the direction of J.R. Fewlass.

Staff of H.A.L., J.R. Fewlass, second from left. A Hull-London service was established in 1970 flying Britten Norman Islanders from Brough to Leavesden near Watford, but the construction of the 600ft chimney at the nearby Capper Pass smelting works prevented further development of this service.

A float at Hull's Lord Mayor's parade, King Edward Street, advertising Humber Airways and the multitude of other branches including Tranby Printers (a development of the old Wilson printing works), Castle Craft which catered for the yachtsman and Easons Travel Agency. After expansion into a helicopter service for the North Sea offshore oil industry suddenly, in 1978, the Ellerman board decided to pull out of aviation completely.

MV *Destro* launched at Floro, Norway, in June 1970. She was 329ft (100m) long, 1,571 tons gross, a twin-screw, stern-loading vessel and container carrier with twin funnels; the three hundred and sixty fifth vessels to have sailed in the Wilson fleet. She and the *Domino* were ordered to replace the lift-on, lift-off container ships in the Norwegian trade. *Domino* replaced *Spero* on the Gothenburg run.

MV *Hero*, under construction at the Robb-Caledon yard, Leith, she was launched in June 1972, length 343ft (105m) and 3,468 tons, a twin-screw stern-loading, motor vehicle and container carrier. She was jointly owned by E.W.L. and D.F.D.S. in the Hull-Esbjerg service carrying bacon and dairy produce from Denmark.

MV *Hero*. In February 1973 the Esbjerg service, still using *Hero*, was transferred to Grimsby. The *Spero* was withdrawn from service and sold to Greek owners as the *Sappho*. She had never fulfilled the high hopes of a profitable cargo-passenger trade. In 1978, the last sailing of a Wilson vessel from Hull was the departure of *Destro* on 29 September to new owners in Italy.

BIRD'S EYE VIEW OF THE TOWN OF KINGSTON-UPON-HULL.

This and the following picture demonstrate the changes of nearly a hundred years. Pettingell's Birds Eye View, 1881. From left to right; the Town Docks system, the double-decked pier for the Hull-New Holland river ferry (now superseded by the Humber Bridge) Victoria Dock, Earles shipyard and the extreme western end of Alexandra Dock, the last and biggest (53 acres; 21.44ha) of the nineteenth century docks, not opened until 1885.

King George Dock, 1964. As vessels became bigger, new and larger docks were built for them to the east of the town, Victoria Dock 1850, Alexandra Dock, 1885, and in 1914 the King George V Dock was opened by his Majesty – 62 acres (25.1ha) and the first dock in the country to use electric power. This is the scene prior to the era of containerisation with fourteen cargo vessels being handled on quayside berths with traditional dock cranes, or discharging into lighters, like the ship on the north side beyond the Blue Star vessel (extreme right).